Ella Frears was born in Truro and grew up in St Ives. Her collection *Shine, Darling* (Offord Road Books, 2020) was shortlisted for the Forward Prize for Best First Collection, and the T. S. Eliot Prize for Poetry. She has been poet in residence for Tate Britain, the National Trust, Royal Holloway University physics department, K6 Gallery, and the John Hansard Gallery where she wrote *I AM THE MOTHER CAT* (Rough Trade Books, 2021). Ella's poems about the St Ives Modernists were on show at Tate St Ives. In 2022, Ella was named the first ever Poet in Residence for the Dartington Trust's gardens.

Aaron Kent was born in Redruth, Cornwall. He is a working-class writer and publisher, and runs the Michael Marks Publishing Award winning press Broken Sleep Books. Aaron was awarded the Awen medal from the Bards of Cornwall for his poetry pamphlet *The Last Hundred*. His work has been praised by Gillian Clarke, J. H. Prynne, Andrew McMillan, Andre Bagoo, Vahni (Anthony Ezekiel) Capildeo, and John McCulough. His recent books include the full-length collection *Angels the Size of Houses*, and a collaboration with surrealist artist John Welson, *A Requiem for Bioluminescence.*

MODERN POETRIES 1
Cornish Modern Poetries

Edited by Ella Frears & Aaron Kent

—

ISBN: 978-1-915079-75-6

—

brokensleepbooks.com

—

—

Cover designed by Aaron Kent

—

Typeset by Aaron Kent

—

Edited by Ella Frears & Aaron Kent

—

Kernewek Consultant: Taran Spalding-Jenkin

Broken Sleep Books
Rhydwen
Talgarreg
Ceredigion
SA44 4HB

Broken Sleep Books
Fair View
St Georges Road
Cornwall
PL26 7YH

Contents

Modern Poetries 1

Cornish Modern Poetries

from The Girls of Situations

I stayed with a man after work who kept tarantulas in the loft space. I had on my mint deli uniform and my face was grey. I cut cheese all day long and ham on an industrial slicer, I didn't want to see the bastard black legs of the largest tarantula he called it King, it slept in a plastic container with air holes at the top

and my protests were nothing down the rattling metal pull-down stairs he came with the wobbling box in hand, how sad it actually was to see the spider uselessly point his legs in the air as if to sense a threat in this house with a Disney quilt Princess frieze for his 6-year-old daughter who stays each Saturday, we don't talk about her, he hides the spiders when she comes around, I am not enough to have them hidden for, the blanket of my apron is a pouch for King in the dirt of his kitchen I would like to go home.

Walls

An ice cream, an oblong of vanilla
from the café on the clifftop in the
gull-squawking, salty gale.

You unwrap the waxy paper
in silence, and I tongue-press
the ice cream into its angular cone,

choose my words carefully,
roll them round in my head
then say the wrong thing, say

nothing, the rain sheeting
between us, the tension dividing
and holding us together.

Cockling

Each moment-met moment
scarcely laps
on muddy Helford shore.

He rose,
tugged on boots palmed
a rusting rake to
scour at the clam's burble.

Breath-held tide
and just a mutter
landed in the greybog
this Cornish Easter.

Minutiae of crabs menace
along barely a
puddle your wellington

death-sentence coquetry
stuck-
tug quick from sludge. Noise

not far of dog. Toddler too.
Inglorious schlork
and freed silting the shells-

their fond distributions.
And from
the clagged bucket a

whisper is heavily
risen.

cabaret

is it haselwort – asarabacca growing
wild spikenard in the levant?

a tray of painted porcelain
in a kind of rush – old chum?

mad metropole parlour cirque
between compté and pinot noir or

pot house – booth – mythic wood and thatch
french version of taberna?

when jill says it's a cabaret
it's a cabaret

but when *they* say it's a cabaret
it's nothing like a cabaret

when jill says it's a cabaret
it's a cabaret

but when they say it's a cabaret
it's nothing like a cabaret

Novacene

The sanguine glow blurs
Tarmac, sticky
Blue bellied flies
Congregate
Your masonry pieces
submerged
in gorse, sunken moors
Pothole shaped
Memories
A white lorry drives by the estuary
Flapping wings
homebound
A30 Hayle

Streetlamps
Empty green bus stops
An ex-lover at the bus station
Brooding shadows of doubt
The ginger cat slinks
across the building site
petrol-stained wings
Of the magpies
Powder blue, Phthalo Green,
Purple agapanthus
A roundabout

St Michael's mount
Sea mist
The smell of anesthetic
Hospital gloves
Follow the signposts back
To a slow death
The kiss of the day lingers
And for a moment
The edges of the world soften

Bryan Wynter's Landscape, Zennor

The dark is the sea that has soaked through,
dripping into buckets already full –
night-time in the day;
the granite blackened, the fields dimmed,
the moon in each headlight.
With each stroke of the paddle,
you tried to keep time with the sea –
the blue pulling you deeper
into the undertow. In the gallery,
my small body of water
rests in front of your canoe:
your final form, unmoored.

Positive Erosion

Where land slipped, sea thrift thrives
in the ribbons of cliff, providing
a new habitat for the Glanville Fritillary,
nutrient-rich – the fall underneath
Keep Away, an attempt by the council
to keep beachcombers at bay.

Peninsularity — The Land

Rocks, the bones of this landscape
as slow moving as a great animal
sleeping with its back to the wind
exhaling within its ancient breath
vapour that was stilled
deep below seams of arsenic and tin.

A furze of yellow echoes the sun
like butter on the tongue on bright days
when you walk alone over the carn
the land ankle-deep in the ocean
its skirts lifted and a petticoat of lace
frothing where the water turns and turns.

Black basalt stacks the northern edge
a palisade against the quickening tide
blue elvan and greenstone, metamorphic
but cupped mid-pour in the ladle of time
slipping from the land as you scramble down
spiked on sloes that stop your fall.

Big seas and even bigger skies
stretch your horizons far beyond the land
as it crumbles to the south
edging ever northwards in a tilt of the earth
where you walk as the mist drifts in, and holds you
pressed against the ground.

zen orzennor
o zennorzen o
no zen orzennor
norzennorzen
zennorzen zen

Railway Shed Sonnet

bloody good job, that
whoever did that

long low
the Long Rock
it mirrors
the beach its minty green
break waves, foam white grey
above sun behind
fugitive gleam through the steam of a fret rolling fast smudging
shed sea and sand green band frame
musical colour, impressionist hand; and

from my window back home on the hill, I wonder how come a
bloody great industrial shed can
disappear in beautiful insignificance.

Dismyk 60 (a'n Hensowsnek)

Yth esen vy ryb an mor, yn morrep tewesek,
My a driga yn ogas fos mor, gans gwreydh furv,
Ha pur voghes tus a'm gweli owth adhvesi,
Ha'y trigen ow honan yn tyller kernhwili,
Mes pub dydh y hwari genev an tonnow du
Ow tinewi y'm kerghyn. Ny brederis
My dhe allos leverel dhe'n dus heb ganow
Hag yn hel medh keskewsel gans geryow.
Marthus yw ha pur goynt mar ny wodhowgh
Fatel veu furvyes gans an poynt kollell
An fordh dhe dhanvon messajys privedh,
Pan wrug an kreftor sley ow bleyn lymm.
An dhew ahanan a yll kevrenna messaj,
Ha nagonan ken a wor dalgh agan geryow.

Ow Kyjya yn Kernow

An glaw yw tew hag yth esa hanter kammneves
a-ugh an treth glyb; gorr dha leuv a-berth y'm gwlanek.

My a gerdhas a-dro dhe'n gwithti leel kanskweyth
hag ervira bos an ki gwalghys munys,
henwys *an byghanna ki y'n bys*, fug.

Amm dhymm yn pastiji gans oll an fornow byw.

My a synsis oy nowydh tomm war vargen tir ha prederi war gyjya.
My a synsis kanker glas muyns yn palv ow leuv.

My a dennas ow breghel a-ugh ow besyes ha terri linasen
ha'y gwaska orth briansen maw kepar ha kledha.

Lows ow eskisyow y'n stretyn na ha'm drehevel yn hweg war'n
arghow atal.

Howl an myttin ow splanna ow tos hag ow tos
ha'n fleghes havysi yw parys gans aga helern melyn.

A wre'ta jy perthi kov an omglewans a balas toll dres an jydh
gans pal plastek hepken dhe vires orth y leunhe gans an mor?

My a'n mynn yndella – kepar ha dowr ow tava y hyns
dres amal. Kepar ha diw vleujen an mor rudhwyn yn pollen,
lies breghow ow kwevya yn transyek.

Kepar ha'n eythin a leski a-dreus dhe'n gonyow ha'th vos
tarosvan pyskador mayth yw pupprys kas an dor.

Roughtor and Brown Willy

Cairn capped and coven met,
Two hills squat and share the sky,
Pot-kettled and steep with feeling.
Rumbling with the discontent,
Of mountain minded molehills.
But curlew called and livestock led,
They hold hands in the foothills,
Pregnant with the nests of birds,
Speckle egged on horsehair beds,
Song hidden and thriving.
Cave riddled, bower bound,
They're spiderwebbed with fiddleheads,
Hiding neolithic farmyards,
Standing stones and buried crowns.
History to hang your hat on.
Beast prowled and granite peaked,
Eagle nests for buzzards to crow from,
Past last bastions of English eerie.
They watch from giant hand cupped seats
As a country falls into sea.

Sam Horton

A I R

Never draw in blue biro,
you can't erase your mistakes.
She yelled.

In that sticky blue I boldly wrote A I R below the embroidered swoosh.
This was no mistake,
now, they were real.

Got the Nikee's on today then?
He's noticed my trainers.
30 years has passed,
I've come to say goodbye.

This time the A I R is real.
No A I R, no entry.
I've been accepted.

I don't want my kids to have shit trainers,
he said, *they'll get the piss taken out of them at school.*

Three days later, he was gone.

Wish you were here

Summer holidays in the caravan.
Winters still washing cars in the snow.

A makeshift clubhouse on a petrol station forecourt.
An office, with a view.

Geezers love treacle,
but treacle is a sticky word.
Duckers, divers. The uncertain, lost and
looking.

Under the bonnet of a 1989 XR3i,
these men are solid.

As ice melts, the rose tint rimes.
I clock a rusted wing, bald tyre and the

drip,

drip,

drip,

of a puddling leak.

Overalls and grease, cheap suits and leather shoes.
Biscuits dunked into mugs of half-truths,
crumble like far away sand castles
in a fog of Café Crème.

Here they huddle, the package holiday bar.

This is the (a) life.

Mineshafts under foot,
driving golf balls at a gorse covered desert.
Lost forever,
or a hole in one?

We piss against a tree.

Alright treacle?
The test drive is over.

Yes. One lady owner from new. Full service history,
and 12 months MOT.

The postcard read,
I wish you were here.

MAEN EGLOS, LIZARD PENINSULA

Held in the dazzling gaze of the sun's noon eye
this vast uneasy sea moves at the wind's whim,
waves cresting ceaselessly, pronouncing again and again
in a frenzy of exultation, the mile-long presence
of *Maen Eglos*, treacherous, half-hidden graveyard,
ships and souls all going down, down, hundreds
year upon year, drowning within sight of St Keverne's
octagonal spire: daymark of his burial ground, daymark of hers.

Stret Meur

--ha lowen
lowr dhe'm daskor / My a gavas teylu

aral / Venezwela trigys wosa-Hungari /
i a'm res tarosvan / mires orthiv owth

omwolghi hwath / dha ji yw kothhes /
an fos tellek gans bili / an lowarth

las dre vras
plosek / ev o yndellma kyns / dha lagatta

a dhrehevis My yn pub stevel / an poos
a'n kommol / pellkanon rag tewedh keser /

ty avel kowr / a'm gwelas ow koska rag own
y hwelsen vy an krakkys / my a's gwel lemmyn /

--Krakkyav
/ y krakkyav vy an lughesennow /

Pitch

after Charles Wright

Standing with my back to the wall, goalposts drawn on
in chalk. Knees bent, palms open—ready for the slap,
the prickling skin, a small victory. Jordan yells
he's only good in goal if you kick it straight at him.

I want to be as beautiful as a flooded quarry
I want to be quick, swifter than the turn of a roebuck's head
I want to be strong, muscular, blooming
I want to be bruised and told that I am brave

And every mouth will open to scream my name
And they will carry me on their shoulders like they carry hurt
And we will win but I will never get better
And the locker room walls will crumble, until we see the sky

Cheesewring, Bodmin Moor

Sculpted by wind and rain, giant ovoids poise;
A layer-cake of rock, balancing precariously.
Beside me, on the top-most slab, my granite
Cushion, a strange depression: a concavity
Scoured out by erosion. A few inches across. In it,
Water from last night's storm and a single stone,
Rotating, round and round, whirled by each fitful
Gust. It made a just perceptible rustling sound.

Who put it there? Was it recently?
Another trekker like me? On purpose?
Or pure whimsy? It'll never be known,
But it was working nicely it would seem.
The rim was becoming almost undercut.
A few more hundred thousand years in turn
Of frost and sun, will find a way to force a split
And take the whole ten-ton colossus down.
Things I read in a schoolboy book on geology
Begun to happen before my eyes, as if to mock
My insignificance in the bigger scheme.
In this emptiness it's all too easy to feel gloomy.
I look around for company. But the only sign
Of human presence is behind, on Caradon:
That red light glowing on the television mast.

My gaze turns then to four wild ponies watering
At a pond hacked out of the ground last century
When people came by the score to labour in a quarry.
They know neither that these men were here before
Nor, that now they're dead and gone. Oblivious
To history, horses live on, untroubled by the past.

Peter Lloyd Jones

Facebooking the boy I first had sex with

'First squid of the year'
is the caption
his dirty fingers squeezing
its translucent neck
over the deck of the boat.
I wish my arms
looked so toned and muscular,
I should do some press-ups.

His penis when it went in me
was fine.
I think I was trying it on
like a dress, just to see.
Maybe now. Or now.
This time?
Does it suit me yet?

Tinder Bio

The child in these photos
isn't mine,
it doesn't belong to me.
But I am using it here
like the carp across my arm,
the tiger drugged for Instagram
and the dog my ex-girlfriend bought
to show you
I am a kind person,
I am the kind of person who
doesn't eat children,
not even one little bit,
wouldn't dream of it.

This photo of its face,
plump and smiling,
uncensored next to mine,
is for you.
This child could be my niece,
or my neighbour,
it really doesn't matter.
You only need to know, that
I am a kind person,
I am the kind of person who
doesn't eat children,
not even a little bit,
wouldn't dream of it.

No, I just pose them on my shoulders
and take them to the park,
and in this photo here,
the child really brings out the blue of my eyes,
don't you think?

There are only two things you need to know:
I am a kind person; I am the kind of person who
doesn't eat children.
and also,
I am using the child for scale.
You see, I'm 6ft 3',
and that seems to be important to you all.

We had a shop

Church Road shop,
Ernie Diamond's shop,
another shop down at Trewellard.

We had a petrol station out at Portheras Cross,
petrol station opposite the Radjel,
another one down at Carnyorth.

Each of these places
had shops
in them.

Bardhonek May Hwisk Hi Ynno Hy Fows Dhemmedhyans Meurgerys

hag yw kesunyans a vor hag a ydhyn.
Yma syns oll a-dro dhedhi. Hern ha brithel
a dernij a-dhiworth roesow ewynek a'y goelesennow.
Ha hi ow tevera, yma lies cher dhe'n bows –
moy es pali, moy es owrlin.
Pows kryghys yw, pows may neuvir ynni,
pows hag ynni re erel a bys. Pows yw
a neb bri, pows a dhirol
der hy diwvregh, a gugh hag a dhiskudh hy fenn.
Ha tergh an mordid ow kildenna, paloresow a fast aga neyth
yn hy gols gwynsek, aga diwarr dhergh ha'ga gelvin
owth afina. Homm yw pows rag karjel ha fyll.
Homm yw pows rag hager-awel – pows owrek ha gwynn,
ha glas ha rudh, ha du. Y'n bows ma,
hi a omglew hanter-Kristones, ow krysi
y'n henwyn koth – an re kerys,
an re kellys – Alef, Cadoc, Dungarth, Salomon.
Ha'n debron erbynn hy kroghen, hi a as
dhe goedha an gwias, ow tos ha bos henhwedhel. Tirwel.

The Way the Crocodile Taught Me

I swooned at the large god of him, sunning.
A tooth for every day of my life.
He performed his run along the bank,
as males do. I brought my boat closer.
He took to following, at a distance.

I wasn't taken in, knew his four-chambered heart
pumped love out and in, in and out,
knew his tongue had few good uses,
knew all about his grin. Yet whoever said he was cold-
blooded has never truly known this beast.

He brought out the prehistoric in me. I dived.
We swam, belly to belly, to where the Niles meet,
tussled as we thrashed among the weeds. After, I lay
the length of him, a limestone lilo, studs patterning
my skin. He smiled at me, often. Taught me all he knew.

Years later, when a man tried to drag me under,
I practised the force my lover had held back –
levered my small jaws open to their furthest extent,
splashed them down on the human's arm.
My attacker still carries the mark of my smile.

The Water Clock

At Poley's Bridge the river's rushing
it's late for the sea
it slides, a smooth brown snake in a hurry.

We're ambling on a sky-blue day
past the abandoned dries now decorated
the faded colours of graffiti tags.

We linger over badger tracks,
horseshoe marks, fading footprints.
These days run on a different clock

like the Tower of the Winds in Roman Athens
water filling re-filling its chambers
gearing clicking night and day

as though the wind can read the time
even with eight strong deities.
Here I want wade in the water

anoint/baptise myself in the old way
immerse myself in the same river twice.

Hensbarrow Down

for Jack Clemo

Late in the day and spears of light
pierce the rain-shadow over Whitemoor.
Rooks circle, head for home
beneath an unlocked sky.

Up here they still speak of a singing stone,
telling the time, tolling the future in a lost tongue.

Just take the old road over the top
all the way down to Menacuddle,

you can hear it ring like tinnitus
pitched on the edge of perception,

singing. singing,
clinging like clay

for this a land where giants walked
and slumber on in their granite bed

under Hensbarrow Down.

The Moor Horses

We race from the top of Kilmar Tor
to see them gallop across the plateau, manes flying, tails

streaming behind, as they plunge into the water
and stand there cooling while foals roll on the grass.

And still the horses arrive, as if they've descended
from petroglyphs, released from millennia carved on walls,

tracing the water-scent, the ancestral map to this pool
set in the slope like a gem-framed black mirror.

They are frost and flint hooved, the appaloosa stallion
splashed with sparks from bonfires in the great caverns.

His mare erupts from the mud
and glares at us, her eyes dusted with rock sleep.

Hasn't she just woken from stone dreams? Doesn't her pearl coat
with its bronze paint tell us she is sacred?

And isn't your blood free as a feral pony, coursing
through the uplands of your body? Your bones granite,

your marrow clear as the brooks that thread down to the valleys.
The months that we trekked up through the ruins

and you photographed each stonechat and lark,
our picnics under fruiting rowans, then up

to the top of the tor, with its stone formations
like fertility goddesses. And that last hot day when

the horses appeared, and flew beneath Bearah Tor.
Their blessing, when the whole moor raised itself to the sky

like a shield to protect us. That moment when you
held out your hand and touched the stallion – as if you too

were made of porphyry and quartz that had just sprung to life.

Got Into Difficulties

meant little more than newspeak
until one hot afternoon
just a wave stretch
from a Cornish beach.

There he turned on my boy and me
shocked in the course of fun.
Briefly testing our souls for ripeness
before dumping us back on the sand
like two sprawls of tide junk.

Now when I hear it said again
I know that grip.
Can see him in his pit
checking the ledger
to draw a bony finger along my entry
with a thin patient smile.

awaiting positive

five days
and one sweaty long walk
familiar giggles blaring out of
tinny brick phones

the ocean, she's turquoise today
complimenting a pink eight o'clock sunrise
and a grinning orange haired friend
at the door.

the air isn't so crisp
but white sepia skies
feel bright compared to artificial warm lights.

another day another bedroom
another bell pepper
or two
chopped
with the knife
stuck in my gate.

too many old tupperwares
sit naked in the rack
airing themselves off
after their bath.

i long for sleep
my back aches
and my eyes tire
as i shut down
the laptop again

3 Years 7 Attempts

Pretending it's ok
mid-stream in chaos
won't wash with my friends.

Hearing our children's silence
in the gaps between battles
cuts through excuses.

Sleeping in a cold car
on nights I'm locked out
fuels my resolve.

Having my head stitched
at eight in the morning
unravels me.

Seeing my clothes
rain down from an upstairs window
precipitates my leaving.

Closing the door
on a long dead marriage
sets us free.

Boz Lenow

Liw ow len
yw glas a gler yn-lowen,
ha golow glan an myttin
ow sydhla dre dhel a sen.

Kroft ha krann
avorow a vydh gwydhlann,
hel avel blasow henwin
lev gwenyn may liv yn-bann.

Selyow sur
yn kel yn grond an kesur:
lyr a lever y gevrin
yntra meyn a furvya mur.

Yn koedh y kow an haz mil greyth
y'n gwerez leyth yntra meyn ha grow,
mes kan avorow a vleuzyow yn-leyth.

Decidual cast

like the meat of a snail scooped out
from the shell and plopped into brine
sinew folds the inside of a cat's ear
large and pink and fleshy

for a moment I thought it was fertilised
and look I know that wouldn't really change much
and I wouldn't have wanted it anyway

but there's something about the body escaping the body
the inside showing itself out the door
deconstructing the threshold in its wake

baby remember you are looking at
a hunk of biological material
that has been dunked in toilet
water it's like reading tea leaves
(not to be insensitive)

I waste little pieces of myself on everything I touch
skin cells on yellow handrails of the bus
hairs trailed breadcrumbs through the trees

sometimes I think I would like
to leave something discernible behind
like a fifty-foot cast iron sculpture of my tits
or a venetian canal with the exact scent of my skin

maybe what I'm trying to say is that this body
will outlive me in ways I can't imagine
beyond categorisation
watery and seething

Marina Scott

washing the lips

once I thought
I knew more about death
than all the ancient Egyptians put together

more than those two mourners
in the Cartier-Bresson photo
mother and son
watchful and cowed
as minor royalty

more than a hunting owl
or a lioness with whelps to feed
or Mary Queen of Scots

more than battlefields
ghosts and coroners

some of us mourn
by the washing of the lips
          let the dead one taste water for the last time
some by wearing a garment in the child's favourite colour
some by amputating a little finger
or hiring a funeral stripper

death?
I hadn't even begun

London of London child

great copper dome of The Planetarium
whinnies and shies as she scootles out of the kerbed-Bentley

child doesn't notice   being in a hurry
dashes up to the sandwicherie at the top

starts counting the many tiny down-there people
who walk along the streety paving stones

window-shopping for the nice-to-haves   till everyone vanishes
in a catchmeifyoucan of erl-kings   back to their toy theatre world

and bother there's no orca pod up here after all they were just joking her
where to now? growls Madame Two-Swords

from deepdown in the plush cenote of the car's interior
as the child temper-tantrums in full-scale dancing octopus mode

and the bendy bus frowns at the Bentley blocking its way
where to, Missy?

A-Barth Estrenyon

Ny glewav vy ow lev.
My a wel ow hanow
war'n reknow ryb an daras
kepar dell didhynnargh.

My a dreylya dhe geunys
dasdewi ow hist lev
lytherennek ow leski
kepar ha Glasnedh.

My a govha skol, ena
nyns yw koweth ow ganow
arwaskus yn y glapp
minhwarthow gans an son

a garnow war'n fordh dhu
ow tasseni yn ow klopen.
Ny allav vy prederi yn ow liwyow
rudh ha gwynn hepken.

My a gelli dens dell taves nowydh
herdhya yn-mes ow briansen.
My a gyv an dens ma
keskarys y'n ponn, hwath.

Ev a'm kompel dhe henwel
ow Mammwynn henwyn ankoth;
Grandma, granny, nan
geryow leverys dh'y bejeth nevra.

Mes, a-barth estrenyon
yndella re bo.

Hedhyw,
ny glewav vy an yeth
mes, my a yll redya an arwodhyow
ha'n chiow ow theylu, ha'n hwedhlow

a'n tir may trehevsons.
Ena, ni a vrath an dor
orth y verkya gans agan dens
rag nevra vynitha.

Yn despit dhe'n rol an re varow
skrifys yn dha dhorn
my a glewav vy ow lev
pan my a gews.

At the Minack

15th September 2017

Cyrano speaks of death,
I think, but the rain—

I catch
the shadow, the double

in wait
since Arras, since

this morning
miles away

when someone left a bag
on the tube,

when someone set a fuse.
My sister

at my side
at the Minack,

my sister
on that line,

day in,
day—

Murmured news
by now

in hospital
waiting rooms.

The axis
of another life

tilts, re-sets.
But the light

here in Mount's Bay,
backdrop of Cyrano's

drenched end, winks,
winks again.

Thankful for this:
my sister

at my side,
the words

of others
that speak

in all
this pain.

Grandmother's jug

A cup-your-hands, curl-your-fingers
cradle-it sphere, rounded and rising
to flared mouth and pouting lip —
a satisfying shape
for storing and pouring.

Tin-smudged colours of Cornish cliffs,
this jug's so shiny I can see my face in it
stretched like the strange mirrors at a fair,
square chest, high head, strong nose —
look what this jug does to me.

If I stare long enough I can see
my grandmother kneading
and baking, spooning and straining,
pouring tea for everyone
until she is all poured out.

Threshold

I've painted my front door the colour of putty,
filled it with glass, etched its panes with tiny stars.
Now light can cross between
in and out, before and after, then and now.

When you left it was solid black,
shaking the house when it banged shut.
Nowadays it opens and closes quietly.
On my terms.

Woman, cliff, islands

On the cliff edge
in a white-washed cottage
clinging to the ancient rock
she felt years spread under her feet;
strata of muted colours
threaded here and there
with ribbons of gold.

She knew that she would live
precariously, weaving
her stories into song;
Tregeseal, Cape Cornwall, Lamorna
faded tapestries of childhood
made bright again.

Now the roof of the cottage
is ablaze with sunlight
and from a bedroom window
you would see the fog lifting,
a woman walking in the valley
and beyond the sea's horizon
the delicate embroidery
of distant islands.

St Kew Highway Services

A midway station
a modest affair
pulling in to see
to a flickering reserve
less crisis - more absence
of thought
or thinking of pausing
taking your finger
off the trigger - seeing
how long before
you can't go back
to filling up – and what point
it decides you're done - the fam
wonder what is taking you
so long - it's not the choice
of crisps - or queue
for the single loo
or tap you leave to run
longer than you need to
it's not even the payment
failure of one of your cards
for no reason - turns out
you've been gone years
every tenner of petrol
- a decade.

A Curse

They were turned to stone | we were told
for making merry on the Sabbath |
Those merry maidens | the standing stones

Children | like us | bussed in to believe
that heaven | like earth | held a place
for those who obeyed | These rules

carved into rock | beside a sign | no littering
But a plastic bag snatched at my boot
and caught in the turf | A form that flowers

and chokes | Swept up white around my legs
A frozen pillar | A plastic statue in the snow
queen's palace | And it spread like grayscale

this gift-wrap petrifaction | a choking ash
for the micro-fibred dogs of Pompeii | asleep
under an explosion of false pumice

I am the child caught in the Gorgon's
cellophane gaze | seduced with ease | And if
I owned this mirror | could I live with beer

yoked in hi cone bricks | birds caught in a mesh
of clay | whales weighed down with granite
crap | If I was born to know no better

Fat Years

Our shop was known for the home-cooked hams
my father bagged with honey and spice,
floated in the blackened sarcophagus
of the haybox to simmer overnight,
the flame lowered to a blue flutter
as he fitted the stainless-steel lid,
sealing its edges with canvas wads.

After chapel, he'd break open the tomb,
slump a ham on the marble counter,
nick its cellophane bag with the tip
of a knife, the ham juice spurting
like water struck from stone, a gush
he'd catch in a handleless mug he handed
to me, the fat a golden scurry as I drank.

Alternative Father #1

In Sunday School, with the 'Uncle'
who tested milk at the dairy,
we looked into Creation
through the big brass microscope
he'd brought in for Pentecost
in a black wooden case.

It was tarnished like a trumpet,
old as the foxed engravings
of Wesley in the Men's Room.
He said, no artist, even Leonardo,
made anything as beautiful
as a bird's nest. I stood on a chair

to gaze through its peephole at water
he'd collected from the pond
where we sailed our boats on Good Friday,
my eye a blank disk of light
guillotined by his slide,
its spasming stained-glass insurgence,

all bite and fuck and filament,
devouring what heavenly light
of Christ was left in my heart's
wild loud beating,
the green-jewelled watch
unhinged, springs and escapements

tumbling through cold light—
I grasped the microscope
and knocked the jar off the table,
its dark shout flung across
the upper room's bare boards
while they all sang on in the faraway chapel.

Cornwall Blue(s)

The tuning
device
of the morning
picks up
A440,
the yellow heart
of a violin
emits
modulations
until
dusk.

Acknowledgements

Rachael Allen's poem *from 'The Girls of Situations'* excerpted from *Kingdomland* (Faber, 2019)

Sarah Barr's poem Walls appeared first on the Poetry Society website.

Jennifer Edgecombe's poem Bryan Wynter's *Landscape, Zennor* appeared first in *The Grief of the Sea* (Broken Sleep Books, 2021).

Christopher Lanyon's poem *Pitch* appeared first in *swell* (Bad Betty, 2022).

Jaime Lock's poem *Facebooking the boy I first had sex with* appeared first in Impossible Archetype #11.

Katrina Naomi's poem *The Way the Crocodile Taught Me* appeared first in The Way the Crocodile Taught Me (Seren, 2016).

Katrina Naomi's poem *Bardhonek May Hwisk Hi Ynno Hy Fows Dhemmedhyans Meurgerys* was translated into Kernewek from Katrina's English original *Poem in Which She Wears Her Favourite Wedding Dress* by Katrina Naomi and Steve Penhaligon. It appeared first in Wild Persistence (Seren, 2020)

Pascale Petit's poem *The Moor Horses* appeared first in the TLS.

Katherine Stansfield's poem *At the Minack* appeared first in We Could Be Anywhere By Now (Seren, 2020).

Vivienne Tregenza's poem *Woman, cliff, islands* previously published in *Invisible Borders (New Women's Writing from Cornwall)* by Hypatia Publications. Published in 'the simple things' UK women's national magazine, November 2020.

Contributors

Rachael Allen was born in Cornwall and studied at Goldsmiths College. She is the co-author of Jolene, a book of poems and photographs with Guy Gormley, and Nights of Poor Sleep, a book of poems and paintings with Marie Jacotey. She has received a Northern Writers' Award and an Eric Gregory Award, and was made a Faber New Poet in 2014. She is poetry editor at Granta and co-founder of the poetry press clinic and online journal tender.

Sarah Barr writes poetry and fiction, teaches creative writing, works as a mentor for writers, and leads a Poetry Society Stanza group. Her poems have appeared in a range of print and online publications including The Frogmore Papers, The New European, and in The Bridport Prize Anthologies. Among the prizes won by her poems are first in the Frogmore Poetry Prize 2015 and the National Memory Day poetry competition 2018. Her poetry pamphlet, January, was published in 2020. Her short story collection is forthcoming in 2022.

Caspar Bryant is a poet from West Cornwall and has lived there all his life. He writes poetry inspired by the sea, digital spaces, chaos, and ars poetica. He studies at St. Andrews University and is currently working on a pamphlet about strange women and miracles. Caspar often misses the Atlantic, especially the walks around Rinsey, Gurnard's Head – all of Graham-country – and Lamorna. Cornish Modern Poetries is his first foray into the wider poetry world beyond a variety of campus publications.

David Devanny is a multi-media artist, writer and researcher. He holds a PhD in Publishing Studies from Falmouth University where he is a Senior Lecturer in English, Writing & Publishing. David's print work has been published in a wide variety of magazines and anthologies, and in his pamphlet Wasps on the Way (Mews Press: 2012). His multimedia text artworks have been presented and exhibited widely including at Husk Arts Centre, The Hatton Gallery and the Prado Media Lab.

Chloé Eathorne is a Cornish poet, journalist and radio presenter born and raised in Redruth. She has had previous work published in FOREGROUND magazine. She is currently studying Creative Writing and Journalism at Falmouth University. In her spare time, she presents The Wildflower Hour for her local community radio station. She is passionate about mental health and wellbeing, which she discusses regularly on the show, together with art and poetry, alongside introducing music from local artists.

Jennifer Edgecombe grew up in Camborne, Cornwall and now lives on the Kent coast. Her debut poetry pamphlet The Grief of the Sea published in 2020 from Broken Sleep Books. Her poems have appeared in Ambit, Lighthouse, PN Review and Wild Court, and featured in Carcanet's New Poetries VIII anthology in 2021.

Gilla Evans is a translator and writer living in the far west of Cornwall. Originally from the New Forest, she has also lived in cities (Sheffield, Aberdeen, Granada, Lisbon and Paris) for varying lengths of time. She has a degree in modern languages and has translated 40/50 books, mainly non-fiction (largely art and architecture), and has worked for leading European art galleries and museums. She has worked collaboratively with a leading Chilean poet and several other Spanish and Portuguese poets.

Andrew Fentham lives in Penryn. His most recent poetry pamphlet is Hunglish (Broken Sleep, 2019). He runs The Grammarsow, a project enabling early-career Scottish poets to visit Cornwall in the footsteps of WS Graham.

Penny Florence is Professor Emerita at The Slade School of Fine Art. The seas and ancient sites of West Penwith, where she has lived for over 30 years, have taught her the meaning of home. She has published widely on poetry and painting, and on feminism. Railway Shed Sonnet is only her second poem in print. She has a collection of poems coming out next year with Beir Bua press.

Ivor Frankell lives in Cornwall with his wife in Carbis Bay, having retired from teaching English Literature and Media Studies in a Jewish school in Manchester several years ago after an episode of throat cancer. He divides his time between writing, reading, language study, and wandering about Cornwall with his camera. His writing explores identity, history and language.

Sam Horton trained as a costume designer and worked in theatre, tv and film before turning to visual arts and illustration. He has always been drawn to landscapes, and to folklore, both as a visual artist and a writer. And now, living in the shadow of the twin peaks of Bodmin Moor, uses his work to try and express his thoughts about the Cornish countryside and his place in it. Sam was highly commended in the Hammond House International short story prize and was shortlisted in the flash fiction category at the 2020 Bridport Prize.
Liam Jolly is an artist, musician and music promoter born, raised - and now based again - in Redruth, Cornwall, where he also runs Auction House, an artist led project and exhibition space.

Alice Kavounas studied English Literature At Vassar and is a tutor with The Poetry School London. Her poems have appeared in The Poetry Review, London Magazine, TLS, New England Review, and in several anthologies, including Out of Fashion, edited by Carol Ann Duffy (Faber, 2004), and Accompanied Voices, edited by John Greening (The Boydell Press, 2015), Her latest collection, Abandoned Gardens, Selected and New Poems, is soon to be followed by One Step at a Time, both published by Shearsman Books.

Christopher Lanyon is a poet and mathematician from Cornwall, living in Nottingham. His poems have been published in Ambit, Abridged, SPOONFEED, Finished Creatures & Under the Radar, among others. His debut pamphlet, swell, is available from Bad Betty Press.

Peter Lloyd Jones trained first as a scientist at Imperial College and then Kings College Cambridge. He then turned to painting via a spell at the Slade School, London. This led to a career mostly in teaching: first at Wimbledon School of Art and then as Head of Design at Kingston University. On his retirement he returned to Cornwall and set up his studio in the Tamar Valley. Peter first came to know Cornwall as an evacuee from London at the outset of the Second World War.

Jaime Lock (they/them) is a poet and script writer from the Isles of Scilly, now based in East London. Jaime was a BBC New Creative, an Apples and Snakes 2021 Writers' Room member and is part of Cornwall New Writers network. They have poems in Signal House Edition, Giving Room Mag and the anthology 26 Voices for Change, among others. Jaime also sings sea shanties.

Jodie Matthews is a Cornish writer and poet, currently living in the north. Her debut novel, *Meet Me At The Surface*, set on Bodmin Moor is forthcoming from 4th Estate in 2024.

Callum Mitchell has produced work for National Trust, Bristol Old Vic, The Lit, & more. His first radio work, *Solomon Browne*, was broadcast on BBC Radio 4 to mark the 40th anniversary of the Penlee lifeboat disaster and is available via the BBC Sounds app. He collaborates with filmmaker Mark Jenkin, and was Assistant Director on the BAFTA-winning *Bait* as well as the forthcoming *Enys Men*. An Associate Artist at Hall For Cornwall, he was the recipient of the Nick Darke Talent Award 2020, and a member of the BBC Writers room Cornish Voices programme 2021.

Katrina Naomi is the winner of the 2021 Keats-Shelley Prize. Katrina's most recent collection, Wild Persistence, (Seren, 2020), received an Authors' Foundation award from the Society of Authors. Same But Different, with Helen Mort, (Hazel Press, 2021) won the 2022 Saboteur Awards. The Way the Crocodile Taught Me (Seren, 2016) was a #FoylesFiveForPoetry and received an Arts Council award. Her poetry has appeared on Poems on the Underground, BBC Radio 4's Front Row, and in The TLS, The Poetry Review and Modern Poetry in Translation.

David Penhale was born in Port Talbot of Welsh-Cornish parents, and raised in Fowey. In the late 70's played music professionally for 3 years with the Cornish singer, Brenda Wootton, touring extensively in Europe and Australia. Awarded by the Red River Poetry Competition, commended for both the Poetry Society and Charles Causley Competitions; latest pamphlet 'Landfall' published by Indian King Poets(2021).

Pascale Petit was born in Paris and lives near Bodmin Moor in Cornwall. She is of French, Welsh, and Indian heritage. Her eighth collection, Tiger Girl (Bloodaxe Books, 2020), was shortlisted for the Forward Prize and for Wales Book of the Year. A poem from the book won the Keats-Shelley Prize. Her seventh collection, Mama Amazonica (Bloodaxe Books, 2017), won the inaugural Laurel Prize for eco-poetry, the RSL Ondaatje Prize, was shortlisted for the Roehampton Prize and was a Poetry Book Society Choice. In 2018 she was elected as a Royal Society of Literature Fellow.

Henry Purbrick is a retired Coastguard living in Penryn having had an interesting career which included tying knots in sausages, monitoring radiation on an experimental nuclear reactor and running his own tea-shop. His poetry collection 'Aim High' is due for publication in the autumn of 2022.

Eggy Ray is a queer, non-binary poet based in Falmouth and Penzance. It is through the practices of walking and writing, often paired together, that they find a place to reflect and understand the millions of silly little thoughts running around their head. The Cornish landscape tends to be one of the main inspirations for theirpoems; both the rural, rugged spaces and the concrete, grey cobbled streets that they find their words.

Fi Read has called Penzance home for 23 years - the same amount of time she's been involved with Penzance's Acorn Theatre. The perfect introduction to the local performing arts and music scene, Fi spent more than a decade promoting and reviewing cultural events as a freelance contributor for Cornwall Today magazine, and other publications, as well as through her weekly Community Spirit column in the Cornishman newspaper.

Tim Saunders is a Cornish poet and journalist primarily writing in the Cornish language who also writes in the Welsh, Irish, and Breton languages. He is resident in Cardiff but is of Cornish descent. He is a bard of the Gorsedh Kernow, a literary historian and editor of 'The Wheel' – an anthology of modern poetry in Cornish 1850–1980. High Tide is a collection of his own poems in Cornish from the years 1974 to 1999.

Marina Scott is a writer who grew up in Falmouth by the sea. They are currently based in South East London, where they work remotely as an assistant programmer for a literary festival and study MA Creative and Life Writing at Goldsmiths. With work concerned with gender, ecofeminism, and (anti)capitalism, they hold a degree in English Literature from the University of Cambridge and have published work with Sticky Fingers Publishing, SPAM Zine, Polyester Zine, Antithesis Journal and Lucy Writers Platform.

Penelope Shuttle has received a Gregory Award and a Cholmondeley Award. Redgrove's Wife, (Bloodaxe Books, 2007), was shortlisted for the T S Eliot Award, and for The Forward Prize. Shuttle is President of the Falmouth Poetry Group, founded in 1972 by her late husband, poet Peter Redgrove. She is widely published, has read at many festivals and venues, and has broadcast her work. Her radio poem, Conversations on a Bench, set in Falmouth, was heard on BBC Radio 4 in March 2020, and she is a contributor to The Verb on Radio 3.

Taran Spalding-Jenkin is an award-winning poet and storyteller who uses English and his mother tongue, Kernewek, to explore identity, health and hireth through the lens of folklore. Since 2019 he has co-organised and hosted Tonic, Bristol's music and poetry party, and has facilitated bilingual creative workshops with schools and community groups across the South West. In 2021 Broken Sleep Books published his Legitimate Snack A Tongue Too Long. A Shanty For Cornish Youth won a Creativity award from Gorsedh Kernow in 2021.

Katherine Stansfield grew up in the village of St Breward on Bodmin Moor and now lives in Cardiff. She has published two full length poetry collections and a pamphlet with Seren. The most recent is We Could Be Anywhere By Now which explores relationships between Cornwall and Wales along personal and linguistic lines. The book was supported by a writer's bursary from Literature Wales and was selected by Wales Literature Exchange as a 'Bookcase' title: a book from Wales recommended for translation.

Anne Symons was born and raised in Truro. She began writing poetry in 2015 at the age of 70. Her work has appeared online and in print publications including Agenda, Alchemy Spoon, Dreamcatcher, Ekphrastic Review, Ink Sweat & Tears, Orbis, Poetry Salzburg Review and The Atlanta Review (Cornwall and Wales edition, Spring 2020). She recently completed an MA in Writing Poetry at Newcastle University and the Poetry School in London.

Anne Taylor is a writer and teacher who has lived in Cornwall for more than 20 years. She worked for many years as a journalist and then lecturer at Falmouth University before developing a career as a group facilitator specialising in therapeutic and reflective writing, and turning to writing poetry. She won second prize in the international Cornwall Contemporary Poetry Festival competition in 2018 and her poems have appeared in the pamphlet Uneasy Heads and on Poetryandcovid.com.

Vivienne Tregenza is an award-winning Cornish poet, well published in poetry journals and anthologies. She is working towards a first collection.

Trelawney is a food campaigner and poet shortlisted and commended in the recent Bridport and Winchester Poetry Prizes respectively; a finalist in the Munster Literature Centre's International Chapbook Competition 2022; and has work published or forthcoming in Ink, Sweat and Tears, The Madrigal, the Alchemy Spoon, Dawntreader and elsewhere. Twitter: @BenTrelawney - Insta.BenTrelawney

John Wedgwood Clarke was born and raised in St Ives, Cornwall. He has published two full collections of poems Ghost Pot (2012) and Landfill (2017). A new collection, Boy Thing, is forthcoming from Arc in 2023. He is currently leading a poetry project about the Red River in West Cornwall www.redriverpoetry.com funded by the Arts and Humanities Research Council, and a senior lecturer in creative writing at the University of Exeter.

Aysegul Yildirim is a writer and researcher. Her debut poetry pamphlet, Plants Beyond Desire, is forthcoming with Broken Sleep Books. Her writing has appeared in The Maynard, Beir Bua, Strukturriss, Sonic Field, The Babel Tower Notice Board and elsewhere. She had her work shortlisted for Streetcake Innovative Writing Prize 2021. As of 2022, she is a final year PhD candidate in Sociology at Goldsmiths University of London and working on a second book.

APERTYA DHA ANKRES

Ingram Content Group UK Ltd.
Milton Keynes UK
UKHW010802130323
418477UK00005B/930